SWEATERS
for Men™

General Information

Many of the products used in this pattern book can be purchased from local craft, fabric and variety stores, or from the Annie's Attic Needlecraft Catalog (see Customer Service information on page 25).

Tunisian Rib Stitch
Zip Front Cardigan

SKILL LEVEL

EXPERIENCED

FINISHED SIZES
Instructions given fit 34–36-inch chest *(small)*; changes for 38–40-inch chest *(medium)*, 42–44-inch chest *(large)*, 46–48-inch chest *(X-large)* and 50–52-inch chest *(2X-large)* are in [ ].

FINISHED GARMENT MEASUREMENTS
Chest: 40 inches *(small)* [44 inches *(medium)*, 47 inches *(large)*, 49 inches *(X-large)*, 52 inches *(2X-large)*]

MATERIALS
- Caron Simply Soft medium (worsted) weight yarn (6 oz/330 yds/170g per skein):
  6 [7, 8, 9, 10] skeins #9750 chocolate
- Sizes J/10/6mm and K/10½/6.5mm afghan hooks or size needed to obtain gauge

- Size J/10/6mm crochet hook
- Tapestry needle
- Sewing needle
- 30 [30, 32, 34, 34]-inch separating zipper (excess length will be cut off)
- Stitch markers
- Straight pins
- Matching sewing thread
- Optional nail polish or fabric glue

GAUGE
With size K afghan hook: 14 sts = 4 inches; 14 rows = 4 inches

PATTERN NOTE
Weave in ends as work progresses.

SPECIAL STITCHES
Tunisian knit stitch (tks): With yarn in back of work, insert hook to right of next vertical bar to

Figure 1
Tunisian Knit Stitch

back of work (see Fig. 1), yo, draw lp through.

Tunisian purl stitch (tps): Bring yarn to front of work, insert hook under next vertical bar, yo

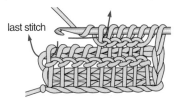

Figure 2
Tunisian purl stitch

(see Fig. 2), draw lp through.

INSTRUCTIONS
BACK
Row 1 (RS): With size K afghan hook, ch 71 [79, 83, 85, 91], insert hook in 2nd ch from hook, yo, draw lp through, *insert hook in next ch, yo, draw lp through, rep from * across (70 [78, 82, 84, 90] lps on hook), to work lps off, ch 1, **yo,

draw through 2 lps on hook, rep from ** until 1 lp rem on hook.

Row 2: Ch 1, sk first vertical bar, *tks (see Special Stitches), tps (see Special Stitches), rep from * across, to work lps off, yo, draw through 1 lp on hook, *yo, draw through 2 lps on hook, rep from * until 1 lp rem on hook.

Rep row 2 until piece measures 19 [19½, 20, 20½, 21] inches from beg.

Note: Mark last row at both sides for armhole.

Rep row 2 until armhole measures 9½ [10, 11, 11½, 12½] inches.

SHOULDER SHAPING
Note: On following rows, both shoulders are worked at same time.

FOR SIZES SMALL, LARGE, X-LARGE & 2X-LARGE ONLY
Row 1: Ch 1, sk first vertical bar, [tks, tps] 12 [14, 14, 15] times, tks (26 [30, 30, 32] lps on hook for first shoulder), drop yarn, join 2nd skein of yarn, insert hook to right of next vertical bar to back of work, yo, draw lp through, bring yarn to front of work, insert under next vertical bar, yo, draw 2 lps on hook, bring yarn to back of work, **insert hook to right of next vertical bar to back of work, yo, draw through 2 lps on hook, bring yarn to front of work, insert under next vertical bar, yo, draw 2 lps on hook, bring yarn to back of work, rep from ** 7 [10, 11, 12] times, [tps, tks] 13 [15, 15, 16] times (26 [30, 30, 32] lps on hook for 2nd shoulder), to work lps off, yo, draw through 1 lp on hook, *yo, draw through 2 lps on hook, rep from * until 1 lp rem on hook.

Row 2: Ch 1, sk first vertical bar, *tks, tps, rep from * across to last 2 vertical bars, insert hook under last 2 vertical bars, yo, draw lp through (25 [29, 29, 31] lps on hook), on next shoulder, insert hook under first 2 vertical bars, yo, draw lp through, **tks, tps, rep from ** across (25 [29, 29, 31] lps on hook), to work lps off, yo, draw through 1 lp on hook, ***yo, draw through 2 lps on hook, rep from *** until 1 lp rem on hook for each shoulder.

Row 3: Ch 1, sk first vertical bar, *tks, tps, rep from * across to last 2 vertical bars, insert hook under last 2 vertical bars, yo, draw lp through *(24 [28, 28, 30] lps on hook)*, on next shoulder, insert hook under first 2 vertical bars, yo, draw lp through, **tks, tps, rep from ** across *(24 [28, 28, 30] lps on hook)*, to work lps off, yo, draw through 1 lp on hook, ***yo, draw through 2 lps on hook, rep from *** until 1 lp rem on hook for each shoulder.

Rows 4 & 5: Rep row 3. *(22 [26, 26, 28] lps on hook for each shoulder at end of last row)*

Row 6: Ch 1, sk first vertical bar, *tks, tps, rep from * across, to work lps off, yo, draw through 1 lp on hook, *yo, draw through 2 lps on hook, rep from * until 1 lp rem on hook.

Rep row 6 until armhole measures 10 [11½, 12, 13] inches.

Last row: Ch 1, sk first vertical bar, *insert hook under next vertical bar, yo, draw through 2 lps on hook, rep from * across. Fasten off.

FOR SIZE MEDIUM ONLY

Row [1]: Ch 1, sk first vertical bar, [tks, tps] [14] times *([29] lps on hook for first shoulder)*, drop yarn, join 2nd skein of yarn, with yarn in front of work, insert under next vertical bar, yo, draw 2 lps on hook, with yarn in back, insert hook to right of next vertical bar to back of work, yo, draw through 2 lps on hook, bring yarn to front of work, insert under next vertical bar, yo, draw 2 lps on hook, bring yarn to back of work, rep from ** [7] times, insert hook to right of next vertical bar to back of work, yo, draw through 2 lps on hook, [tps, tks] [28] times *(29 lps on hook for 2nd shoulder)*, to work lps off, yo, draw through 1 lp on hook, *yo, draw through 2 lps on hook, rep from * until 1 lp rem on hook for both shoulders.

Row [2]: Ch 1, sk first vertical bar, *tks, tps, rep from * across to last 2 vertical bars, insert hook under last 2 vertical bars, yo, draw lp through *([28] lps on hook)*, on next shoulder, insert hook under first 2 vertical bars, yo, draw lp through, **tks, tps, rep from ** across *([28] lps on hook)*, to work lps off, yo, draw through 1 lp on hook, ***yo, draw through 2 lps on hook, rep from *** until 1 lp rem on hook for each shoulder.

Rows [3–5]: Rep row [2]. *([25] lps on hook for each shoulder at end of last row)*

Row [6]: Ch 1, sk first vertical bar, *tks, tps, rep from * across, to work lps off, yo, draw through 1 lp on hook, *yo, draw through 2 lps on hook, rep from * until 1 lp remains on hook.

Rep row 6 until armhole measures [10½] inches.

Last row: Ch 1, sk first vertical bar, *insert hook under next vertical bar, yo, draw through 2 lps on hook, rep from * across. Fasten off.

RIGHT FRONT

Row 1 (RS): With size K afghan hook, ch 36 [40, 42, 43, 46], insert hook in 2nd ch from hook, yo, draw lp through, *insert hook in next ch, yo, draw lp through, rep from * across *(35 [39, 41, 42, 45] lps on hook)*, to work lps off, ch 1, **yo, draw through 2 lps on hook, rep from ** until 1 lp rem on hook.

FOR SIZES SMALL, MEDIUM, LARGE & 2X-LARGE ONLY

Row 2: Ch 1, sk first vertical bar, *tks, tps, rep from * across to last vertical bar, tks, to work lps off, yo, draw through 1 lp on hook, *yo, draw through 2 lps on hook, rep from * until 1 lp rem on hook.

Rep row 2 until piece measures 19 [19½, 20, 21] inches.

Note: Mark last row at left side for armhole.

Rep row 2 until armhole measures 6 [6½, 7, 8] inches.

SHOULDER SHAPING

Row 1: Ch 1, sk first vertical bar, [insert hook under next vertical bar, yo, draw through 2 lps on hook] 6 times, [tks, tps] 14 [16, 17, 19] times *(29 [33, 35, 39] lps on hook)*, work lps off, yo, draw through 1 lp on hook, *yo, draw through 2 lps on hook, rep from * until 1 lp rem on hook.

Row 2: Ch 1, sk first vertical bar, insert hook under next 2 vertical bars, yo, draw through 2 lps on hook, *tks, tps, rep from * across *(28 [32, 34, 38] lps on hook)*, to work off lps, **yo, draw through 2 lps on hook, rep from ** until 1 lp rem on hook.

Rows 3–8 [3–9, 3–10, 3–11, 3–12]: Rep row 2. (22 [25, 26, 26, 28] *lps on hook at end of last row*)

Work even in established pattern until armhole measures 10 [10½, 11½, 13] inches.

Last row: Ch 1, sk first vertical bar, *insert hook under next vertical bar, yo, draw through 2 lps on hook, rep from * across. Fasten off.

FOR SIZE X-LARGE ONLY
Row [2]: Ch 1, sk first vertical bar, *tks, tps, rep from * across to last vertical bar, to work lps off, yo, draw through 1 lp on hook, *yo, draw through 2 lps on hook, rep from * until 1 lp rem on hook.

Rep row 2 until piece measures [20½] inches.

Note: Mark last row at right side for armhole.

Rep row 2 until armhole measures [7½] inches.

SHOULDER SHAPING
Row [1]: Ch 1, sk first vertical bar, [insert hook under next vertical bar, yo, draw through 2 lps on hook] 6 times, [tks, tps] [17] times, tks ([36] *lps on hook*), work lps off, yo, draw through 1 lp on hook, *yo, draw through 2 lps on hook, rep from * until 1 lp rem on hook.

Row [2]: Ch 1, sk first vertical bar, *tks, tps, rep from * across to last 2 vertical bars, yo, draw lp through ([35] *lps on hook*), to work lps off, *yo, draw through 2 lps on hook, rep from * until 1 lp rem on hook.

Rows [3–11]: Rep row [2]. ([26] *lps on hook at end of last row*)

Work even in established pattern until armhole measures [12] inches.

Last row: Ch 1, sk first vertical bar, *insert hook under next vertical bar, yo, draw through 2 lps on hook, rep from * across. Fasten off.

LEFT FRONT
Work same as Right Front, reversing shaping.

SLEEVE
MAKE 2.
RIBBING

Row 1: With size J afghan hook, ch 37 [37, 41, 45, 47], insert hook in 2nd ch from hook, yo, draw lp through, *insert hook in next ch, yo, draw lp through, rep from * across (36 [36, 40, 44, 46] *lps on hook*), to work lps off, ch 1, **yo, draw through 2 lps on hook, rep from ** until 1 lp rem on hook.

Row 2: Ch 1, sk first vertical bar, *tks, tps, rep from * across, to work lps off, yo, draw through 1 lp on hook, *yo, draw through 2 lps on hook, rep from * until 1 lp rem on hook.

Rep row 2 until piece measures 2 inches from beg. Change to size K afghan hook.

BODY
Row 1: Ch 1, sk first vertical bar, insert hook under back lp of next st, yo, draw lp through (*inc made*), tks in same st, tps, *tks, tps, rep from * across to last 2 vertical bars, tks, insert hook under back lp of next st (*inc made*), yo, draw lp through, tps (37 [41, 43, 44, 47] *lps on hook*), to work lps off, yo, draw through 1 lp on hook, *yo, draw through 2 lps on hook, rep from * until 1 lp rem on hook.

Working in established pattern and working inc sts into pattern, inc 1 st at each end of every 3rd row 6 [8, 9, 9, 10] times, then every 4th row 10 [10, 10, 11, 11] times. (70 [74, 80, 86, 90] *lps on hook at end of last row*)

Work even until piece measures 19½ [20, 21, 21½, 22] inches 68 (70, 74, 76, 77) rows from Ribbing.

Last row: Ch 1, sk first vertical bar, *insert hook under next vertical bar, yo, draw through 2 lps on hook, rep from * across. Fasten off.

ASSEMBLY
Steam Back, Fronts, and Sleeves lightly and pin to cutting board to conform to measurements on schematics. Allow to dry. Sew Fronts to Back along shoulder seams.

COLLAR
Row 1: With WS facing and with size J afghan hook, join yarn in corner of Left Front, draw up 6 lps evenly sp along Left Front center neck edge, 16 [17, 17, 18, 19] lps evenly sp across Left Front side neck edge, 3 lps evenly sp across

left back shoulder edge, 18 [20, 22, 24, 26] lps evenly sp across back neck, 3 lps across right back shoulder edge, 16 [17, 17, 18, 19] lps across Right Front side neck edge, 6 lps evenly sp across Right Front center neck edge *(68 [72, 74, 78, 82] lps on hook)*, to work lps off, yo, draw through 1 lp on hook, *yo, draw through 2 lps on hook, rep from * until 1 lp rem on hook.

Row 2: Ch 1, sk first vertical bar, *tks, rep from * across, to work lps off, yo, draw through 1 lp on hook, *yo, draw through 2 lps on hook, rep from * until 1 lp rem on hook.

Rep row 2 until piece measures 3 inches.

Last row: Ch 1, sk first vertical bar, *insert hook under next vertical bar, yo, draw through 2 lps on hook, rep from * across. Fasten off.

ASSEMBLY
Sew Sleeves in armholes, easing to fit. Sew side and Sleeve seams.

EDGING
Hold piece with RS facing and starting ch of Back at top, join yarn at right side seam, ch 1, sc in each st to lower corner of Right Front, 3 sc in corner st, working across Right Front, sc in ends of rows, sc evenly sp around Collar, sc in ends of rows down Left Front, 3 sc in lower corner of Left Front, sc in each st across lower edge to beg sc, join with sl st in beg sc. Fasten off.

FINISHING
Pin zipper to Right Front, making sure Cardigan is centered on zipper. With sewing needle and matching thread, sew zipper to Cardigan. Pin Left Front to zipper, butting edges of Cardigan together. Sew left side of zipper to Cardigan. With zipper open, trim excess from top of zipper, dabbing lightly with clear nail polish or fabric glue to inhibit fraying. Tack upper edges of zipper to Cardigan. Tack over ends of zipper teeth creating zipper stops. ∎

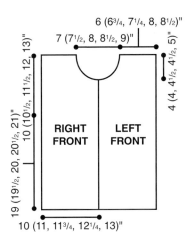

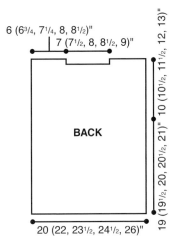

Cabled Jacket

SKILL LEVEL

INTERMEDIATE

FINISHED SIZES
Instructions given fit 34–36-inch chest *(small)*; changes for 38–40-inch chest *(medium)*, 42–44-inch chest *(large)*, 46–48-inch chest *(X-large)* and 50–52-inch chest *(2X-large)* are in [ ].

FINISHED GARMENT MEASUREMENTS
Chest: 40 inches *(small)* [44 inches *(medium)*, 47 inches *(large)*, 49 inches *(X-large)*, 52 inches *(2X-large)*]

MATERIALS
- Caron Simply Soft medium (worsted) weight yarn (6 oz/ 330 yds/170g per skein): 8 [9, 9, 10, 11] skeins #9707 dark sage
- Size I/9/5.5mm crochet hook
- Tapestry needle
- Sewing needle
- 9 dark green ⅞-inch flat buttons
- Stitch markers
- Straight pins
- Matching sewing thread
- Optional nail polish or fabric glue

GAUGE
18 sts and 10 rows = 4 inches

PATTERN NOTES
Weave in ends as work progresses.
Join with a slip stitch unless otherwise stated.

INSTRUCTIONS
BACK
RIBBING
Row 1 (RS): Ch 92 [98, 104, 110, 116], dc in 3rd ch from hook *(beg 3 sk chs count as a dc)*, dc in each rem ch across, turn. *(90 [96, 102, 108, 114] dc)*

Row 2: Ch 2, **fpdc** *(see Stitch Guide)* around first dc, *bpdc *(see Stitch Guide)* around each of next 2 dc, fpdc around next dc, rep from * across to last 2 dc, bpdc around next dc, fpdc around last dc, turn.

Row 3: Ch 2, fpdc around first st, bpdc around next st, *fpdc around next st, bpdc around each of next 2 sts, rep from * across to last st, fpdc around last st, turn.

Rep rows 2 and 3 until piece measures 2 inches from beg, ending with a WS row.

BODY
Row 1 (RS): Ch 2, dc in each of first 6 [9, 3, 6, 9] sts, fpdc around each of next 6 sts, [dc in each of the next 3 sts, fpdc around each of next 6 sts] 8 [8, 10, 10, 10] times, dc in each of last 6 [9, 3, 6, 9] sts, turn.

Row 2: Ch 2, dc in each of first 6 [9, 3, 6, 9] dc, bpdc around each of next 6 sts, [dc in each of next 3 dc, bpdc around each of next 6 sts] 8, [8, 10, 10, 10] times, dc in each of last 6 [9, 3, 6, 9] dc, turn.

Row 3: Ch 2, dc in each of first 6 [9, 3, 6, 9] dc, sk next 3 sts, **fptr** *(see Stitch Guide)* around each of next 3 sts, working behind fptr just made, fptr around each of 3 sk sts, [dc in each of next 3 sts, sk next 3 sts, fptr around each of next 3 sts, working behind fptr just made, fptr around each of 3 sk sts] 8 [8, 10, 10, 10] times, dc in each of last 6 [9, 3, 6, 9] dc, turn.

Row 4: Ch 2, dc in each of first 6 [9, 3, 6, 9] sts, bpdc around each of next 6 sts, [dc in each of next 3 sts, bpdc around each of next 6 sts] 8 [8, 10, 10, 10] times, dc in each of last 6 [9, 3, 6, 9] dc, turn.

Row 5: Ch 2, dc in each of first 6 [9, 3, 6, 9] sts, fpdc around each of next 6 sts, [dc in each of next 3 sts, fpdc around each of next 6 sts] 8 [8, 10, 10, 10] times, dc in each of last 6 [9, 3, 6, 9] sts, turn.

Row 6: Ch 2, dc in each of first 6 [9, 3, 6, 9] dc, bpdc around each of next 6 sts, [dc in each of next 3 dc, bpdc around each of next 6 sts] 8, [8, 10, 10, 10] times, dc in each of last 6 [9, 3, 6, 9] dc, turn.

Rep rows 3–6 until piece measures 15¾ [16, 16½, 17, 17½] inches from Ribbing.

ARMHOLE SHAPING
Row 1: Sl st in each of first 3 [4, 5, 5, 6] sts,

work in established pattern across next 84 [88, 92, 98, 102] sts, leaving last 3 [4, 5, 5, 6] sts unworked, turn. *(84 [88, 92, 98, 102] sts)*

Row 2: Ch 2, dc in each of first 3 dc, work in established pattern across, turn.

Row 3: Ch 2, **dc dec** *(see Stitch Guide)* in first 2 sts, work in established pattern across to last 2 sts, dc dec in last 2 sts, turn. *(82 [86, 90, 96, 100] sts)*

Row 4: Ch 2, work in established pattern across, turn.

[Rep rows 3 and 4 alternately] 1 [2, 3, 5, 5] time(s). *(80 [82, 84, 86, 90] sts at end of last row)*

Work in established pattern until armhole measures 11½ [11¾, 11¾, 11¾, 11¾] inches.

SHOULDER SHAPING
Row 1: Sl st in each of first 6 [6, 6, 6, 6] sts, sc in each of next 6 [6, 6, 6, 6] sts, hdc in each of next 6 [6, 6, 6, 7] sts, dc in each of next 7 [7, 7, 7, 7] sts, fasten off, sk next 30 [32, 34, 36, 38] sts, **join** *(see Pattern Notes)* yarn in next st, ch 2, dc in same st as joining, dc in each of next 6 [6, 6, 6, 6] sts, hdc in each of next 6 [6, 6, 6, 7] sts, sc in each of next 6, [6, 6, 6, 6] sts, sl st in each of last 6 [6, 6, 6, 6] sts. Fasten off.

RIGHT FRONT
RIBBING
Row 1 (RS): Ch 47 [50, 53, 56, 59], dc in 3rd ch from hook *(beg 3 sk chs count as a dc)*, dc in each rem ch across, turn. *(45 [48, 51, 54, 57] dc)*

Row 2: Ch 2, fpdc around first dc, bpdc around next dc, *fpdc around next dc, bpdc around each of next 2 sts, rep from * across to last dc, fpdc around last dc, turn.

Row 3: Ch 2, bpdc around first st, *fpdc around each of next 2 sts, bpdc around next st, rep from * across to last 2 sts, fpdc around next st, bpdc around last st, turn.

Rep rows 2 and 3 until ribbing measures 2 inches from beg, ending with a WS row.

BODY
Row 1: Ch 2, dc in each of first 6 [6, 6, 6, 6] sts, fpdc around each of next 6 sts, [dc in each of next 3 sts, fpdc around each of next 6 sts] 3 [3, 4, 4, 4] times, dc in each of last 6 [9, 3, 6, 9] sts, turn.

Row 2: Ch 2, dc in each of first 6 [9, 3, 6, 9] dc, bpdc around each of next 6 sts, [dc in each of next 3 sts, bpdc around each of next 6 sts] 3 [3, 4, 4, 4] times, dc in each of last 6 [6, 6, 6, 6] dc, turn.

Row 3: Ch 2, dc in each of first 6 [6, 6, 6, 6] dc, sk next 3 sts, fptr around each of next 3 sts, working behind fptr just made, fptr around each of 3 sk sts, [dc in each of next 3 sts, sk next 3 sts, fptr around each of next 3 sts, fptr around each of 3 sk sts] 3 [3, 4, 4, 4] times, dc in each of last 6 [9, 3, 6, 9] dc, turn.

Row 4: Ch 2, dc in each of first 6 [9, 3, 6, 9] sts, bpdc around each of next 6 sts, [dc in each of next 3 dc, bpdc around each of next 6 sts] 3 [3, 4, 4, 4] times, dc in each of last 6 [6, 6, 6, 6] dc, turn.

Row 5: Ch 2, dc in each of first 6 [6, 6, 6, 6] sts, fpdc around each of next 6 sts, [dc in each of next 3 sts, fpdc around each of next 6 sts] 3 [3, 4, 4, 4] times, dc in each of last 6 [9, 3, 6, 9] sts, turn.

Row 6: Ch 2, dc in each of first 6 [6, 6, 6, 6] dc, sk next 3 sts, fptr around each of next 3 sts, working behind fptr just made, fptr around each of 3 sk sts, [dc in each of next 3 sts, sk next 3 sts, fptr around each of next 3 sts, fptr around each of 3 sk sts] 3 [3, 4, 4, 4] times, dc in each of last 6 [9, 3, 6, 9] dc, turn.

Rep rows 3–6 until piece measures 15¾ [16, 16½, 17, 17¾] inches from Ribbing, ending with a WS row.

ARMHOLE SHAPING
Row 1 (RS): Ch 2, dc in each of first 6 [6, 6, 6, 6] dc, work in established pattern across to last 3 [4, 5, 5, 6] sts, leaving last 3 [4, 5, 5, 6] sts, unworked, turn. *(42 [45, 48, 51, 54] sts)*

Row 2: Ch 2, dc in each of first 3 dc, work in established pattern across, turn.

Row 3: Ch 2, dc dec in first 2 sts, work in established pattern across to last 2 sts, dc dec in last 2 sts, turn. *(40 [43, 46, 49, 52] sts)*

Row 4: Ch 2, work in established pattern across, turn.

[Rep rows 3 and 4 alternately] 0 [1, 2, 4, 4] time(s). *(40 [41, 42, 43, 45] sts at end of last row)*

Work in established pattern until armhole

measures 7½ [7¾, 7¼, 7¼, 6¾] inches, ending with a WS row.

NECKLINE SHAPING

Row 1 (RS): Sl st in each of first 6 [7, 8, 8, 9] sts, work in established pattern across, turn. (34 [34, 34, 35, 36] sts)

Dec 1 st at neckline edge every row 9 [9, 9, 10, 10] times. (25 [25, 25, 25, 26] sts at end of last row)

Work in established pattern until armhole measures 11½ [11¾, 11¾, 11¾, 11¾] inches from beg, ending with a RS row.

SHOULDER SHAPING

Row 1: Ch 2, dc in each of next 7 [7, 7, 7, 7] sts, hdc in each of next 6 [6, 6, 6, 7] sts, sc in each of next 6 [6, 6, 6, 6] sts, sl st in each of last 6 [6, 6, 6, 6] sts. Fasten off.

LEFT FRONT
RIBBING

Row 1 (RS): Ch 47 [50, 53, 56, 59], dc in 3rd ch from hook (beg 3 sk chs count as a dc), dc in each rem ch across, turn. (45 [48, 51, 54, 57] dc)

Row 2: Ch 2, fpdc around first dc, *bpdc around each of next 2dc, fpdc around next dc, rep from * across to last 2 dc, bpdc around next dc fpdc around last dc, turn.

Row 3: Ch 2, bpdc around first st, fpdc around next st, *bpdc around next st, fpdc around each of next 2 sts, rep from * across to last st, bpdc around last st, turn.

Rep rows 2 and 3 until ribbing measures 2 inches from beg, ending with a WS row.

BODY

Work same as Body of Right Front to Armhole Shaping.

ARMHOLE SHAPING

Row 1 (RS): Sl st in each of first 3 [4, 5, 5, 6] sts, ch 2, dc in same st as last sl st made, work in established pattern across next 41 [43, 45, 48, 50] sts, turn.

Working in established pattern, dec 1 st at end of every other row 2 [3, 4, 6, 6] times. (40 [41, 42, 43, 45] sts at end of last row)

Work in established pattern until armhole measures 7½ [7¾, 7¼, 7¼, 6¾] inches.

NECKLINE SHAPING

Row 1: Ch 2, work in established pattern across to last 6 [7, 8, 8, 9] sts, leaving rem sts unworked, turn. (34 [34, 34, 35, 36] sts)

Dec 1 st at neckline edge every row 9 [9, 9, 10, 10] times. (25 [25, 25, 25, 26] sts at end of last row)

Work in established pattern until armhole measures 11½ [11¾, 11¾, 11¾, 11¾] inches from beg, ending with a RS row .

SHOULDER SHAPING

Row 1: Sl st in each of first 6 [6, 6, 6, 6] sts, sc in each of next 6 [6, 6, 6, 6] sts, hdc in each of next 6 [6, 6, 6, 7] sts, dc in each of next 7 [7, 7, 7, 7] sts. Fasten off.

SLEEVE
MAKE 2.
RIBBING

Row 1 (RS): Ch 47 [53, 53, 59, 59], dc in 3rd ch from hook (beg 3 sk chs count as a dc), dc in each rem ch across, turn. (45 [51, 51, 57, 57] dc)

Row 2: Ch 2, fpdc around first dc, *bpdc around each of next 2 dc, fpdc around next dc, rep from * across, turn.

Row 3: Ch 2, bpdc around first st, *fpdc around each of next 2 sts, bpdc around next st, rep from * across, turn.

Rep rows 2 and 3 until piece measures 2 inches from beg, ending with a WS row.

BODY

Row 1 (RS): Ch 2, dc in each of first 6 [9, 9, 12, 12] sts, fpdc in each of the next 6 sts, [dc in each of the next 3 sts, fpdc in each of the next 6 sts] 3 [3, 3, 3, 3] times, dc in each of the last 6 [9, 9, 12, 12] sts, ch 2, turn.

Row 2: Ch 2, dc in each of first 6 [9, 9, 12, 12] dc, bpdc around each of next 6 sts, [dc in each of next 3 dc, bpdc around each of next 6 sts] 3 [3, 3, 3, 3] times, dc in each of last 6 [9, 9, 12, 12] dc, turn.

Row 3: Ch 2, 2 dc in first dc, dc in each of next 5 [8, 8, 11, 11] dc, sk next 3 dc, fptr around each of next 3 dc, working behind fptr just made, fptr around each of 3 sk dc, [dc in each of next 3 dc, fptr around each of next 3 dc, working behind fptr just made, fptr around each of 3 sk dc] 3 [3, 3, 3, 3] times, dc in each of next 5 [8, 8, 11, 11] dc, 2 dc in last dc, turn.

Continuing to work in established pattern, inc 1 st at beg and end of every other row 12 [11, 11, 10, 10] times, then every 3rd row 6 [6, 7, 6, 8] times. *(83 [87, 89, 91, 93] sts at end of last row)*

Work even in established pattern until piece measures 17½ [17½, 18, 18, 18] inches from Ribbing.

SHAPE CAP

Row 1: Sl st in each of first 3 [4, 5, 5, 6] sts, work in established pattern in next 77 [79, 79, 81, 81] sts, leaving last 3 [4, 5, 5, 6] sts unworked, turn. *(77 [79, 79, 81, 81] sts)*

Row 2: Ch 2, dc dec in first 2 sts, work in established pattern across to last 2 sts, dc dec in last 2 sts, turn. *(75 [77, 77, 79, 79] sts)*

Working in established pattern, continue to dec 1 st at beg and end of each row 8 [7, 9, 9, 11] times, then dec 2 sts at beg and end of each row 9 [10, 9, 9, 8] times. *(23 [23, 23, 25, 25] sts at end of last row)*

Work in established pattern 0 [0, 1, 1, 1] row. Fasten off.

ASSEMBLY

Steam Back, Fronts, and Sleeves lightly, pin to cutting board to conform to measurements on schematics. Allow to dry before proceeding.

Sew Fronts to Back along shoulder seams. Sew Sleeve Caps in armholes, easing to fit. Sew side and Sleeve seams.

CREW NECK

Row 1 (RS): With RS facing, join yarn at corner of Right Front neck edge, ch 2, work 6 [7, 8, 8, 9] dc evenly sp along Right Front edge, 21 [22, 22, 22, 22] dc evenly sp along right neck edge, 30 [32, 33, 36, 37] dc evenly sp along Back neck edge, 21 [22, 22, 22, 22] dc evenly sp along left neck edge, 6 [7, 8, 8, 9] dc evenly sp along Left Front edge, turn. *(87 [90, 93, 96, 99] dc)*

Row 2: Ch 2, bpdc around first st, *fpdc around each of next 2 sts, bpdc around next st, rep from * across, turn.

Row 3: Ch 2, fpdc around first st, *bpdc around each of next 2 sts, fpdc around next st, rep from * across, turn.

Rows 4 & 5: Rep rows 2 and 3.

Row 6: Rep row 2. Fasten off.

BUTTON BAND

Row 1 (RS): With RS facing, join yarn at lower Right Front corner, ch 1, working across Right Front edge, ch 1, 2 sc in end of each row, turn.

Row 2: Ch 1, sc in each sc across, turn.

Rows 3–5: Rep row 2. At end of last row, fasten off.

BUTTONHOLE BAND

Row 1 (RS): With RS facing, join yarn at Left Front neckline corner, ch 1, working across Left Front edge, ch 1, 2 sc in end of each row, turn.

Row 2: Ch 1, sc in each sc across turn.

Note: Mark placement of 9 buttonholes, evenly spaced, having first buttonhole 2 sts from top and last buttonhole 2 sts from bottom.

Row 3: Ch 1, sc in each of first 2 sts, *ch 4 *(buttonhole)*, sk next 4 sc, sc in each sc to next marker, rep from * 7 times, ch 4 *(buttonhole)*, sk next 4 sc, sc in each of last 2 sc, turn.

Row 4: Ch 1, sc in each sc and in each ch across, turn.

Row 5: Ch 1, sc in each sc across. Fasten off.

FINISHING

Sew buttons to Button Band opposite buttonholes. ■

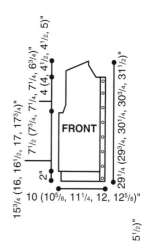

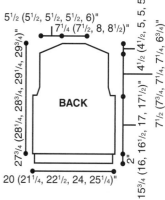

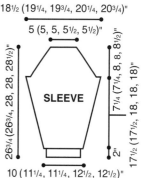

Turtleneck

SKILL LEVEL

INTERMEDIATE

FINISHED SIZES

Instructions given fit 34–36-inch chest (*small*); changes for 38–40-inch chest (*medium*), 42–44-inch chest (*large*), 46–48-inch chest (*X-large*) and 50–52-inch chest (*2X-large*) are in [ ].

FINISHED GARMENT MEASUREMENTS

Chest: 40 inches (*small*) [44 inches (*medium*), 47 inches (*large*), 49 inches (*X-large*), 52 inches (*2X-large*)]

MATERIALS

- Caron Simply Soft Shadows medium (worsted) weight yarn (3 oz/150 yds/85g per skein):
  6 [7, 8, 9, 10] skeins #0005 soft merino
- Size I/9/5.5mm crochet hook or size needed to obtain gauge
- Tapestry needle

GAUGE

16 sts = 4 inches; 10 rows in pattern = 3½ inches
14 dc = 4 inches; 7 dc rows = 4 inches

PATTERN NOTES

Weave in ends as work progresses.
Join rounds with a slip stitch unless otherwise stated.

INSTRUCTIONS
BACK
Note: Back is worked from side to side.

Row 1 (RS): Ch 98 [102, 108, 112, 116], dc in 3rd ch from hook, *sk next ch, dc in next ch, dc in sk ch, rep from * across to last ch, dc in last ch, turn. (*96 [100, 106, 110, 114] dc*)

Row 2: Ch 1, sc in each dc across, turn.

Row 3: Ch 2, dc in first sc, *sk next sc, dc in next sc, dc in sk sc, rep from * across to last sc, dc in last sc, turn.

Rep rows 2 and 3 until piece measures 19 [21, 22½, 24½, 26] inches from beg. At end of last row, fasten off.

Note: Mark 40th [42nd, 46th, 48th, 52nd] st on each side for sleeve placement.

FRONT
Note: Front is worked from side to side.

Row 1 (RS): Ch 98 [102, 108, 112, 116], dc in 3rd ch from hook, *sk next ch, dc in next ch, dc in sk ch, rep from * across to last ch, dc in last ch, turn. (*96 [100, 106, 110, 114] dc*)

Row 2: Ch 1, sc in each dc across, turn.

Row 3: Ch 2, dc in first sc, *sk next sc, dc in next sc, dc in sk sc, rep from * across to last sc, dc in last sc, turn.

Row 4: Ch 1, sc in each dc across, turn.

Rows 5–16 [5–18, 5–20, 5–22, 4–24]: [Rep rows 3 and 4 alternately] 6 [7, 8, 9, 10] times.

LEFT NECKLINE SHAPING
Row 1 (RS): Sl st in each of first 9 [9, 11, 11, 13] sc, ch 2, dc in same sc as last sl st, *sk next sc, dc in next sc, dc in sk sc, rep from * across to last sc, dc in last sc, turn. (*88 [92, 96, 100, 102] dc*)

Row 2: Ch 1, sc in each dc across, turn.

Row 3: Ch 2, **dc dec** (*see Stitch Guide*) in next 3 sc, *sk next sc, dc in next sc, dc in sk sc, rep from * across to last sc, dc in last sc, turn. (*86 [90, 94, 98, 100] dc*)

Row 4: Rep row 2.

Rows 5–10: [Rep rows 3 and 4 alternately] 3 times. (*80 [84, 88, 92, 94] dc at end of last row*)

Rows 11–20 [11–22, 11–24, 11–24]: [Rep rows 3 and 4 alternately] 5 [6, 6, 7, 7] times.

RIGHT NECKLINE SHAPING
Row 1 (RS): Ch 1, sc in each dc across, turn.

Row 2: Ch 4, dc in 3rd ch from hook, sk next ch, dc in next sc, dc in sk ch, *sk next sc, dc in next sc, dc in sk sc, rep from * across to last sc, dc in last sc. (82 [86, 90, 94, 96] dc)

Rows 3–8: [Rep rows 1 and 2 alternately] 3 times. (88 [92, 96, 100, 102] dc at end of last row)

Row 9: Ch 1, sc in each st across, turn.

Row 10: Ch 10 [10, 12, 12, 14], dc in 3rd ch from hook, [sk next ch, dc in next ch] 4 [4, 5, 5, 6] times, *sk next sc, dc in next sc, dc in sk sc, rep from * across to last sc, dc in last sc, turn.

Row 11: Ch 1, sc in each dc across, turn.

Row 12: Ch 2, dc in first sc, *sk next sc, dc in next sc, dc in sk sc, rep from * across to last sc, dc in last sc, turn.

Rows 13–24 [13–26, 13–28, 13–30, 13–32]: [Rep rows 3 and 4 alternately] 7 [8, 9, 10, 11] times.

Rows 25 [27, 29, 31, 33]: Ch 1, sc in each dc across. Fasten off.

Note: Mark 40th [42nd, 46th, 48th, 52nd] st on each side for sleeve placement.

SLEEVE
MAKE 2.
Row 1 (RS): Ch 12, dc in 3rd ch from hook, *sk next ch, dc in next ch, dc in sk ch, rep from * across to last sc, dc in last ch, turn. (10 dc)

Row 2: Ch 1, sc in each dc across, turn.

Row 3: Ch 12, dc in 3rd ch from hook, [sk next ch, dc in next ch, dc in sk ch] 5 times, *sk next sc, dc in next sc, dc in sk sc, rep from * across to last sc, dc in last sc, turn. (20 dc)

Rows 4–13: [Rep rows 3 and 4 alternately] 5 times. (70 dc at end of last row)

FOR SIZES SMALL AND LARGE ONLY
Row 14: Ch 1, sc in each dc across, turn.

Row 15: Ch 10, dc in 3rd ch from hook, [sk next ch, dc in next ch, dc in sk ch] 4 times, *sk next sc, dc in next sc, dc in sk sc, rep from * across to last sc, dc in last sc, turn. (78 dc)

FOR SIZES MEDIUM, X-LARGE AND 2X-LARGE ONLY
Rows [14 and 15]: Rep rows 2 and 3. ([80] dc at end of last row)

FOR SIZES LARGE AND X-LARGE ONLY
Row [16]: Ch 1, sc in each dc across, turn.

Row [17]: Ch 8, dc in 3rd ch from hook, [sk next ch, dc in next ch] 3 times, *sk next sc, dc in next sc, dc in sk sc, rep from * across to last sc, dc in last sc, ch 1, turn. ([84, 86] dc)

FOR SIZE 2X-LARGE ONLY
Row [16]: Ch 1, sc in each dc across, turn.

Row [17]: Ch 10, dc in 3rd ch from hook, [sk next ch, dc in next ch] 4 times, *sk next sc, dc in next sc, dc in sk sc, rep from * across to last sc, dc in last sc, turn. ([88] dc).

FOR ALL SIZES
Row 16 [16, 18, 16, 18]: Ch 1, sc in each dc across, turn.

Row 17 [17, 19, 17, 19]: Ch 2, dc in first sc, *sk next sc, dc in next sc, dc in sk sc, rep from * across to last sc, dc in last sc, turn.

Rows 18–47 [18–47, 20–49, 18–47, 20–49]: [Rep last 2 rows alternately] 15 times.

Row 48 [48, 50, 48, 50]: Ch 1, sc in each dc across, turn.

Row 49 [49, 51, 49, 51]: Ch 2, dc in first sc, *sk next sc, dc in next sc, dc in sk sc, rep from * across to last 8 [10, 6, 6, 8] sc, dc in last sc, leaving rem sc unworked, turn. (70 [70, 78, 80, 80] dc)

Row 50 [50, 52, 50, 52]: Ch 1, sc in each dc across, turn.

Row 51 [51, 53, 51, 53]: Ch 2, dc in first sc, *sk next sc, dc in next sc, dc in sk sc, rep from * across to last 10 [10, 8, 10, 10] sc, dc in last sc, leaving rem sc unworked, turn. *(60 [60, 70, 70, 70] dc)*

Row 52 [52, 54, 52, 54]: Ch 1, sc in each dc across, turn.

Rows 53–62 [53–62, 55–68, 53–66, 55–68]: [Rep last 2 rows alternately] 5 [5, 7, 7, 7] times. At end of last row, fasten off.

ASSEMBLY
Steam Back, Front, and Sleeves lightly, pin to cutting board to conform to measurements on schematics. Allow to dry before proceeding.

Sew Front to Back along shoulder seams.

TURTLENECK
Rnd 1 (RS): With RS facing, join yarn in 1 shoulder seam, ch 2, work 80 [80, 84, 84, 88] dc evenly sp around neckline, **join** *(see Pattern Notes)* in beg dc.

Rnd 2: Ch 2, **fpdc** *(see Stitch Guide)* around each of first 2 dc, **bpdc** *(see Stitch Guide)* around each of next 2 dc, *fpdc around each of next 2 dc, bpdc around each of next 2 dc, rep from * around, join in beg fpdc.

Rnd 3: Ch 2, fpdc around each of first 2 fpdc, bpdc around each of next 2 bpdc, *fpdc around each of next 2 fpdc, bpdc around each of next 2 bpdc, rep from * around, join in beg fpdc.

Rep rnd 3 until piece measures 6 inches from beg or desired length. At end of last rnd, fasten off.

SLEEVE CUFF
Row 1 (RS): With RS facing, join yarn at lower edge of Sleeve, ch 2, working in ends of rows, work 43 [43, 46, 49, 52] dc evenly sp across, turn.

Row 2: Ch 2, bpdc around each of first 2 dc, fpdc around next dc, *bpdc around each of next 2 dc, fpdc around next dc, rep from * across, turn.

Row 3: Ch 2, fpdc in each fpdc, bpdc in each bpdc to end, ch 2, turn.

Rep rows 2 and 3 until piece measures 2 inches from beg. At end of last row, fasten off.

Rep on 2nd Sleeve.

FINISHING
Sew Sleeves in armholes, easing to fit. Sew side and Sleeve seams.

LOWER RIBBING
Rnd 1 (RS): With RS facing and starting ch at top, join yarn at right side seam, ch 2, working in ends of rows, work 75 [84, 87, 96, 99] dc evenly sp across Front and 75 [84, 87, 96, 99] dc evenly sp across Back, join in beg dc.

Rnd 2: Ch 2, fpdc around each of first 2 dc, bpdc around next dc, *fpdc around each of next 2 dc, bpdc around next dc, rep from * around, join in beg fpdc.

Rep rnd 2 until ribbing measures 2½ inches from beg or to desired length. At end of last rnd, fasten off. ∎

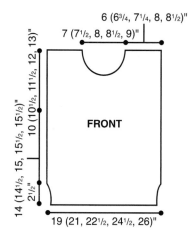

FRONT

6 (6¾, 7¼, 8, 8½)"

7 (7½, 8, 8½, 9)"

14 (14½, 15, 15½, 15½)"

10 (10½, 11½, 12, 13)"

2½"

19 (21, 22½, 24½, 26)"

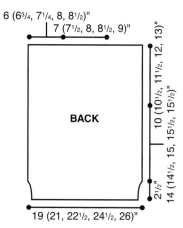

BACK

6 (6¾, 7¼, 8, 8½)"

7 (7½, 8, 8½, 9)"

10 (10½, 11½, 12, 13)"

14 (14½, 15, 15½, 15½)"

2½"

19 (21, 22½, 24½, 26)"

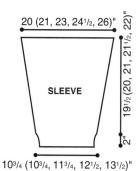

SLEEVE

20 (21, 23, 24½, 26)"

19½ (20, 21, 21½, 22)"

2"

10¾ (10¾, 11¾, 12½, 13½)"

Zip Front
Men's Vest

SKILL LEVEL

INTERMEDIATE

FINISHED SIZES

Instructions given fit 34–36-inch chest (*small*); changes for 38–40-inch chest (*medium*), 42–44-inch chest (*large*), 46–48-inch chest (*X-large*) and 50–52-inch chest (*2X-large*) are in [ ].

FINISHED GARMENT MEASUREMENTS

Chest: 40 inches (*small*) [44 inches (*medium*), 47 inches (*large*), 49 inches (*X-large*), 52 inches (*2X-large*)]

MATERIALS

- NaturallyCaron.com Country medium (worsted) weight yarn (3 oz/185 yds/86g per skein):
  5 [6, 7, 8, 9] skeins #0016 charcoal
  3 [3, 4, 4, 4] skeins #0019 vicuna
- Size H/8/5mm crochet hook or size needed to obtain gauge
- Tapestry needle
- Sewing needle
- 30 [30, 32, 34, 34]-inch separating zipper (excess length will be cut off)
- Stitch markers
- Straight pins
- Matching sewing thread
- Optional nail polish or fabric glue

GAUGE

For Back: 18 dc = 4 inches; 9 rows = 4 inches
For Front: 19 sc = 4 inches; 23 rows = 4 inches

PATTERN NOTES

Weave in ends as work progresses.
Join rounds with a slip stitch unless otherwise stated.
Partial repeats of pattern may be needed in some rows.

INSTRUCTIONS
BACK
RIBBING

Row 1 (RS): With charcoal, ch 86 [94, 102, 110, 118] dc in 3rd ch from hook, dc in each rem ch across, turn. (*84 [92, 100, 108, 116] dc*)

Row 2: Ch 2, hdc in first dc, *__bpdc__ (*see Stitch Guide*) around each of next 2 dc **, hdc in each of next 2 dc, rep from * across, ending last rep at **, hdc in last dc, turn

Row 3: Ch 2, hdc in first hdc, *__fpdc__ (*see Stitch Guide*) around each of next 2 sts **, hdc in each of next 2 sts, rep from * across, ending last rep at **, hdc in last st, turn.

Rows 4 & 5: Rep rows 2 and 3.

BODY

Row 1 (WS): Ch 2, dc in each st across, turn.

Rep row 1 until piece measures 14 [14½, 15, 15½, 15½] inches from beg, ending with a WS row.

ARMHOLE SHAPING

Row 1 (RS): Sl st in each of first 7 dc, ch 2, dc in same dc as last sl st made, dc in each of next 71 [79, 87, 95, 103] sts, leaving rem dc unworked, turn. (*72 [80, 88, 96, 104] dc*)

Row 2: Ch 2, **dc dec** (*see Stitch Guide*) in first 2 dc, dc in each of next 68 [76, 84, 92, 100] dc, dc dec in last 2 dc, turn. (*70 [78, 86, 94, 102] dc*)

Row 3: Ch 2, dc dec in first 2 dc, dc in each of next 66 [74, 82, 90, 98] dc, dc dec in last 2 dc, turn. (*68 [76, 84, 92, 100] dc*)

Row 4: Ch 2, dc dec in first 2 sts, dc in each of next 64 [72, 80, 88, 96] dc, dc dec in last 2 sts, turn. (*66 [74, 82, 90, 98] dc*)

Row 5: Ch 2, dc in each dc across, turn.

Rows 6–27 [6–28, 6–31, 6–32, 6–35]: Rep row 5.

SHOULDER SHAPING
Row 28 [29, 32, 33, 36]: Sc in each of first 6 [7, 8, 9, 10] sts, hdc in each of next 6 [7, 8, 9, 10] sts, dc in next 6 [7, 9, 9, 10] sts, sk 30 [32, 32, 36, 38] sts, attach separate ball of yarn, in next st, ch 2, dc in same space and in next 6 [7, 9, 9, 10] sts, hdc in each of next 6 [7, 8, 9, 10] sts, sc in each of last 6 [7, 8, 9, 10] sts.

Row 28 [29, 32, 33, 36]: Ch 1, sc in each of first 6 [7, 8, 9, 10] dc, hdc in each of next 6 [7, 8, 9, 10] dc, dc in each of next 6 [7, 9, 9, 10] dc, drop yarn, sk next 30 [32, 32, 36, 38] dc, **join** (*see Pattern Notes*) 2nd skein of yarn in next dc, ch 2, dc in same dc as joining, dc in each of next 6 [7, 9, 9, 10] dc, hdc in each of next 6 [7, 8, 9, 10] dc, sc in each of last 6 [7, 8, 9, 10] dc. Fasten off.

RIGHT FRONT
RIBBING
Row 1 (RS): With charcoal, ch 46 [50, 54, 58, 62], dc in 3rd ch from hook, dc in each rem ch across, turn. (*44 [48, 52, 56, 60] dc*)

Row 2: Ch 2, hdc in first st, *bpdc each of next 2 sts **, hdc in each of next 2 sts, rep from * across, ending last rep at **, hdc in last st, turn.

Row 3: Ch 2, hdc in first hdc, *fpdc around each of next 2 sts **, hdc in each of next 2 sts, rep from * across, ending last rep at **, hdc in last st, turn.

Rows 4 & 5: Rep rows 2 and 3.

BODY
Row 1 (WS): Ch 2, 2 sc in first st, sc each st across to last st, 2 sc in last st, **changing color** (*see Stitch Guide*) to vicuna in last sc, turn. (*46 [50, 54, 58, 62] sc*)

Row 2 (RS): Ch 1, sc in each of first 2 sts, ***fptr** (*see Stitch Guide*) around each of next 2 sts, sc in each of next 2 sts, rep from * across, turn.

Row 3: Ch 1, sc in each st across, changing to charcoal in last sc, turn.

Row 4: Ch 1, sc in each of first 2 sts, *fpdc around each of next 2 sts, sc in each of next 2 sts, rep from * across, turn.

Row 5: Ch 1, sc in each st across, change to vicuna in last st, turn.

Row 6: Ch 1, sc in each of first 2 sts, *fpdc around each of next 2 sts, sc in each of next 2 sts, rep from * across, turn.

Row 7: Ch 1, sc in each st across, change to charcoal in last st, turn.

Rep rows 4–7 until piece measures 14 [14½, 15, 15½, 15½] inches from beg, ending with a WS row.

ARMHOLE SHAPING
Note: Work following rows in established color sequence.

Row 1 (RS): Ch 1, sc in each of first 2 sts, *fpdc around each of next 2 sts, sc in each of next 2 sts, rep from * across to last 6 sts, leaving rem 6 sts unworked, turn. (*40 [44, 48, 52, 56] sts*)

Row 2: Ch 1, **sc dec** (*see Stitch Guide*) in first 2 sts, sc in each rem st across, turn. (*39 [43, 47, 51, 55] sts*)

Row 3: Ch 1, sc in each of first 2 sts, *fpdc around each of next 2 sts, sc in each of next 2 sts, rep from * across, turn.

Row 4: Ch 1, sc dec in first 2 sts, sc in each rem st across, turn. (*38 [42, 46, 50, 54] sts*)

Row 5: Ch 1, sc in each of first 2 sts, *fpdc around each of next 2 sts, sc in each of next 2 sts, rep from * across, turn.

Row 6: Ch 1, sc dec in first 2 sc, sc in each rem st across, turn. (*37 [41, 45, 49, 53] sts*)

Continue to work in established pattern until piece measures 21¼ [22¼, 23¼, 24¼, 24¾] inches from beg (including ribbing), ending with a WS row.

NECKLINE SHAPING
Row 1: Sl st in each of first 5 sts, ch 1, sc in

same st as last sl st made, continue to work in established pattern across row. (33 [37, 41, 45, 49] sts)

Row 2: Work in established pattern across row to last 2 sts, sc dec in last 2 sts. (32 [36, 40, 44, 48] sts)

Row 3: Ch 1, sc dec in first 2 sts, work in established pattern across row. (31 [35, 39, 43, 47] sts)

Row 4: Ch 1, work in established pattern across row to last 2 sts, sc dec in last 2 sts. (30 [34, 38, 42, 46] sts)

Rep rows 3 and 4 until 20 [23, 26, 29, 32] sts rem.

Continue to work in established pattern until piece measures 25¼ [26¼, 27¾, 28¾, 29¾] inches from beg, including ribbing. At end of last row, fasten off.

LEFT FRONT
Work same as Right Front, reversing shaping.

ASSEMBLY
Steam Back and Fronts lightly, pin to cutting board to conform to measurements on schematics. Allow to dry before proceeding.

With charcoal, sew Fronts to Back along shoulder seams. Sew Fronts to Back along side seams.

COLLAR
Row 1 (RS): With RS facing, join charcoal in end of first row of Neckline Shaping of Right Front, ch 2, dc in same sp, working around neck opening, work 82 [85, 91, 94, 100] dc evenly sp across to last st of Left Front Neckline Shaping, turn.

Row 2: Ch 2, fpdc in first dc, *bpdc in each of next 2 dc **, fpdc in next dc, rep from * across, ending last rep at **, fpdc in last st, turn.

Row 3: Ch 2, bpdc in first st, *fpdc in each of next 2 dc, bpdc in next dc, rep from * across, turn.

Rep rows 2 and 3 until Collar measures 2 inches from beg. At end of last row, fasten off.

EDGING
With RS facing, join charcoal in lower corner of Right Front, ch 1, sc in same sp, working across Right Front, top of Collar and down Left Front, sc evenly sp across to lower corner of Left Front. Fasten off.

FINISHING
Pin zipper to Right Front, making sure Vest is centered on zipper. With sewing needle and matching thread, sew zipper to Vest. Pin Left Front to zipper, butting edges of Vest together, and making sure rows line up. Sew left side of zipper to Vest. With zipper open, trim excess from top of zipper, dabbing lightly with clear nail polish or fabric glue to inhibit fraying. Tack upper edges of zipper to Vest. With charcoal, tack over ends of zipper teeth creating zipper stops. ■

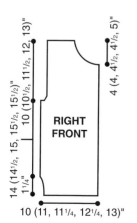
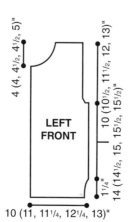
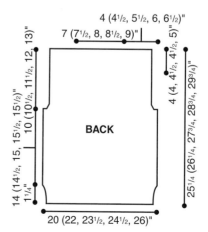

Wave Front Men's Sweater

SKILL LEVEL

INTERMEDIATE

FINISHED SIZES

Instructions given fit 34–36-inch chest (small); changes for 38–40-inch chest (medium), 42–44-inch chest (large), 46–48-inch chest (X-large) and 50–52-inch chest (2X-large) are in [ ].

FINISHED GARMENT MEASUREMENTS

Chest: 40 inches (small) [44 inches (medium), 47 inches (large), 49 inches (X-large), 52 inches (2X-large)]

MATERIALS

- Caron Simply Soft Heather medium (worsted) weight yarn (5 oz/250 yds/142g per skein):
    6 [7, 8, 9, 9] skeins #9508 charcoal heather
    1 skein #9506 deep plum heather (enough for all sizes)
- Caron Simply Soft medium (worsted) weight yarn (6 oz/330 yds/170g per skein):
    1 [1, 1, 2, 2] skein(s) #9742 grey heather
- Size I/9/5.5mm crochet hook or size needed to obtain gauge
- Tapestry needle

GAUGE

15 dc = 4 inches; 9 dc rows = 4 inches
In pattern: 17 sts = 4 inches; 19 rows = 4½ inches

PATTERN NOTES

Weave in ends as work progresses.
Join with a slip stitch unless otherwise stated.
Partial repeats of pattern will be needed in some rows.

INSTRUCTIONS
BACK
BODY

Row 1 (RS): With charcoal heather, ch 68 [75, 81, 88, 93], working in back bars of chs, dc in 3rd ch from hook, dc in each rem ch across, turn. *(66 [73, 79, 86, 91] dc)*

Row 2: Ch 2, dc in each dc across, turn.

Rep row 2 until piece measures 15 [15½, 16, 16½, 16½] inches from beg, ending with a WS row.

ARMHOLE SHAPING

Row 1 (RS): Sl st in each of first 6 dc, ch 2, dc in same dc as last sl st made, dc in each of next 55 [62, 68, 75, 80] sts, leaving rem dc unworked, turn. *(56 [63, 69, 76, 81] dc)*

Row 2: Ch 2, dc in each dc across, turn.

Rep row 2 until piece measures 25 [26, 27½, 28½, 29½] inches from beg. At end of last row, fasten off.

FRONT

Note: Front is worked from side to side in following color sequence: 2 rows charcoal heather, 2 rows grey heather, 2 rows deep plum heather, 2 rows grey heather.

Row 1 (RS): With charcoal heather, ch 65 [67, 69, 71, 71], sc in 2nd ch from hook, sc in next ch, *hdc in each of next 2 chs, dc in each of next 2 chs, tr in each of next 3 chs, dc in each of next 2 chs, hdc in each of next 2 chs, sc in each of next 3 chs, rep from * across, turn. *(64 [66, 68, 70, 70)] sts)*

Row 2: Ch 1, sc in each st across, **changing color** (*see Stitch Guide*) to grey heather in last sc, ch 3, turn.

Row 3: Ch 3, tr in each of first 2 sts, *dc in each of next 2 sts, hdc in each of next 2 sts, sc in each of next 3 sts, hdc in each of next 2 sts, dc in each of next 2 sts, tr in each of next 3 sts, rep from * across, turn.

Row 4: Ch 1, sc in each st across, changing to deep plum heather in last sc, turn.

Row 5: Ch 1, sc in each of first 2 sts, *hdc in each of next 2 sts, dc in each of next 2 sts, tr in

each of next 3 sts, dc in each of next 2 sts, hdc in each of next 2 sts, sc in each of next 3 sts, rep from * across, turn.

Row 6: Ch 43 [45, 47, 49, 49], sc in 2nd ch from hook, sc in each rem ch, sc in each st across, changing to grey heather in last sc, turn. *(106 [110, 114, 118, 118] sc)*

Continue to work in pattern as established and in color sequence as established until there are 9 [11, 11, 12, 13] color stripes, ending with a WS row.

NECKLINE SHAPING

Row 1 (RS): Work in established pattern across first 101 [105, 109, 113, 113] sts, leaving rem sts unworked, turn. *(101 [105, 109, 113, 113] sts)*

Row 2: Ch 1, sc in each st across, turn.

Row 3: Work in established pattern across first 95 [99, 103, 107, 107] sts, leaving rem sts unworked, turn.

Row 4: Ch 1, sc in each st across, turn.

Row 5: Work in established pattern across next 90 [94, 96, 100, 98] sts, leaving rem sts unworked turn. *(90 [94, 96, 100, 98] sts)*

Row 6: Ch 1, sc in each st across.

Row 7: Work in established pattern across, turn.

Row 8: Ch 1, sc in each st across, turn.

Rows 9 & 10 [9 & 10, 9–12, 9–12, 9–12]: [Rep rows 7 and 8 alternately] 1 [1, 2, 2, 2] times.

FRONT OPENING
Row 1 (RS): Work in established pattern across first 78 [82, 84, 88, 86] sts, leaving last 12 sts unworked, turn.

Row 2: Ch 13, sc in 2nd ch from hook, sc in each ch, sc in each st across, turn. (90 [94, 96, 100, 98] sts)

Row 3: Work in established pattern across, turn.

Row 4: Ch 1, sc in each st across, turn.

Rows 5–12 [5–12, 5–12, 5–14, 5–14]: [Rep rows 3 and 4 alternately] 4 [4, 4, 5, 5] times.

LEFT NECKLINE SHAPING
Row 1: Work in established pattern across, turn.

Row 2: Ch 7, sc in 2nd ch from hook sc in each rem ch, sc in each st across, turn. (96 [100, 102, 106, 104] sts)

Row 3: Work in established pattern across, turn.

Row 4: Ch 7, sc in 2nd ch from hook sc in each rem ch, sc in each st across, turn. (96 [100, 102, 106, 104] sts)

Row 5: Work in established pattern across, ch 6 [6, 8, 8, 10]. (5 [5, 7, 7, 9] increases made)

Row 4: Ch 6 [6, 8, 8, 10], sc in 2nd ch from hook sc in each rem ch, sc in each st across, turn. (101 [105, 107, 111, 109] sts)

Continue to work in established pattern for an additional 7 [9, 9, 10, 11] color stripes.

ARMHOLE SHAPING
Row 1: Work in established pattern across next 64 [66, 68, 70, 70] sts, leaving rem sts unworked, turn.

Row 2: Ch 1, sc in each st across, turn.

Row 3: Work in established pattern across, turn.

Row 4: Ch 1, sc in each st across. Fasten off.

SLEEVE
MAKE 2.
RIBBING
Row 1 (RS): With charcoal heather and leaving a 36-inch end, ch 39 [39, 42, 45, 48], working in back bar of chs, dc in 3rd ch from hook, dc in each rem ch across, turn. (37 [37, 40, 43, 46] dc)

Row 2: Ch 2, hdc in first st, *bpdc (see Stitch Guide) around each of next 2 dc, hdc in next st, rep from * across, turn.

Row 3: Ch 2, hdc in first st, *fpdc (see Stitch Guide) around first 2 sts, hdc in next st, rep from * across, turn.

Rep rows 2 and 3 until piece measures 2 inches from beg.

BODY
Row 1: Ch 2, 2 dc in first st, dc in each st across to last st, 2 dc in last st, turn. (39 [39, 42, 45, 48] dc)

Row 2: Ch 2, dc in each st across, turn.

FOR SIZES SMALL & MEDIUM ONLY
Rows 3–34 [3–36]: [Rep rows 1 and 2 alternately] 16 [17] times. Fasten off. (71 [73] dc at end of last row)

FOR SIZES LARGE & X-LARGE ONLY
Rows [3–7]: Rep row 1

Row [8]: Rep row 2.

Rows [9–38]: [Rep rows 1 and 2] [15] times. Fasten off. ([82, 85] dc at end of last row)

FOR SIZE 2X-LARGE ONLY
Rows [3–6]: Rep row 1

Row [8]: Rep row 2.

Rows [9–42]: [Rep rows 1 and 2] [17] times. Fasten off. ([90] dc at end of last row)

ASSEMBLY
Steam Back, Fronts, and Sleeves lightly and pin to cutting board to conform to measurements on schematics. Allow to dry before proceeding. With charcoal heather, sew Fronts to Back along shoulder seams.

NECK RIBBING

Row 1 (RS): With RS facing, **join** (*see Pattern Notes*) charcoal heather in edge of first row of right Front Opening, ch 2, working in ends of rows around neck opening to Left Front Opening, work 79 [79, 82, 85, 88] dc evenly sp across, turn.

Row 2: Ch 2, fpdc around first dc, bpdc around each of next 2 dc, *fpdc around next dc, bpdc around each of next 2 dc, rep from * across to last dc, fpdc in last dc, turn.

Row 3: Ch 2, bpdc around first st, *fpdc around each of next 2 sts, bpdc around next st, rep from * across, turn.

Row 4: Ch 2, fpdc around first st, bpdc around each of next 2 sts, *fpdc around next st, bpdc around each of next 2 sts, rep from * across to last st, fpdc in last st, turn.

Rep rows 3 and 4 until piece measures 2 inches or desired length from beg, ending with a WS row.

EDGING

Ch 2, bpdc around first st, *fpdc around each of next 2 sts, bpdc around next st, rep from * across, working across Front Opening, 2 dc in sp formed by last bpdc made, sc in each of next 12 sts, working across next side, sc in each of next 12 sts, 2 dc in sp formed by beg ch-2, join in beg bpdc. Fasten off.

FINISHING

With charcoal heather, sew Sleeves in armholes, easing to fit. With charcoal heather, sew side and Sleeve seams.

LOWER RIBBING

Rnd 1 (RS): With RS facing and lower edge at top, join charcoal heather in right side seam, ch 2, working in ends of rows across Front, work 66 [74, 80, 85, 92] dc evenly sp across, working in unused lps of starting ch of Back, work 66 [73, 79, 86, 91] dc evenly sp across, join in beg dc. (132 [147, 159, 171, 183} dc)

Rnd 2: Ch 2, fpdc in each of first 2 dc, bpdc in next dc, *fpdc in each of next 2 dc, bpdc in next dc, rep from * around, join in beg fpdc.

Rep rnd 2 until Ribbing measures 2 inches or desired length from beg. At end of last rnd, fasten off. ∎

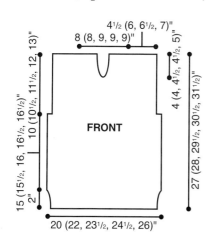

FRONT

4½ (6, 6½, 7)"
8 (8, 9, 9, 9)"
4 (4, 4½, 4½, 5)"
10 (10½, 11½, 12, 13)"
15 (15½, 16, 16½, 16½)"
2"
27 (28, 29½, 30½, 31½)"
20 (22, 23½, 24½, 26)"

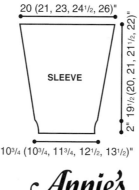

SLEEVE

20 (21, 23, 24½, 26)"
19½ (20, 21, 21½, 22)"
2"
10¾ (10¾, 11¾, 12½, 13½)"

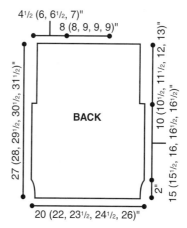

BACK

4½ (6, 6½, 7)"
8 (8, 9, 9, 9)"
10 (10½, 11½, 12, 13)"
27 (28, 29½, 30½, 31½)"
15 (15½, 16, 16½, 16½)"
2"
20 (22, 23½, 24½, 26)"

Annie's Attic®

TOLL-FREE ORDER LINE or to request a free catalog (800) LV-ANNIE (800) 582-6643
Customer Service (800) AT-ANNIE (800) 282-6643, **Fax** (800) 882-6643
Visit anniesattic.com

We have made every effort to ensure the accuracy and completeness of these instructions. We cannot, however, be responsible for human error, typographical mistakes or variations in individual work.

ISBN: 978-1-59635-225-4

Stitch Guide
For more complete information, visit **FreePatterns.com**

ABBREVIATIONS

beg	begin/begins/beginning
bpdc	back post double crochet
bpsc	back post single crochet
bptr	back post treble crochet
CC	contrasting color
ch(s)	chain(s)
ch--	refers to chain or space previously made (i.e. ch-1 space)
ch sp(s)	chain space(s)
cl(s)	cluster(s)
cm	centimeter(s)
dc	double crochet (singular/plural)
dc dec	double crochet 2 or more stitches together, as indicated
dec	decrease/decreases/decreasing
dtr	double treble crochet
ext	extended
fpdc	front post double crochet
fpsc	front post single crochet
fptr	front post treble crochet
g	gram(s)
hdc	half double crochet
hdc dec	half double crochet 2 or more stitches together, as indicated
inc	increase/increases/increasing
lp(s)	loop(s)
MC	main color
mm	millimeter(s)
oz	ounce(s)
pc	popcorn(s)
rem	remain/remains/remaining
rep(s)	repeat(s)
rnd(s)	round(s)
RS	right side
sc	single crochet (singular/plural)
sc dec	single crochet 2 or more stitches together, as indicated
sk	skip/skipped/skipping
sl st(s)	slip stitch(es)
sp(s)	space(s)/spaced
st(s)	stitch(es)
tog	together
tr	treble crochet
trtr	triple treble
WS	wrong side
yd(s)	yard(s)
yo	yarn over

Chain—ch: Yo, pull through lp on hook.

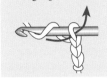

Slip stitch—sl st: Insert hook in st, pull through both lps on hook.

Single crochet—sc: Insert hook in st, yo, pull through st, yo, pull through both lps on hook.

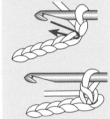

Front post stitch—fp:
Back post stitch—bp: When working post st, insert hook from right to left around post st on previous row.

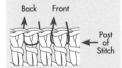

Front loop—front lp
Back loop—back lp

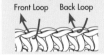

Half double crochet—hdc: Yo, insert hook in st, yo, pull through st, yo, pull through all 3 lps on hook.

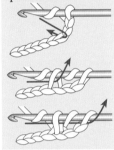

Double crochet—dc: Yo, insert hook in st, yo, pull through st, [yo, pull through 2 lps] twice.

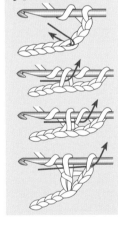

Change colors: Drop first color; with 2nd color, pull through last 2 lps of st.

Treble crochet—tr: Yo twice, insert hook in st, yo, pull through st, [yo, pull through 2 lps] 3 times.

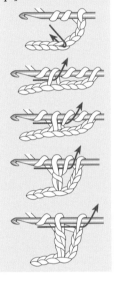

Double treble crochet—dtr: Yo 3 times, insert hook in st, yo, pull through st, [yo, pull through 2 lps] 4 times.

Single crochet decrease (sc dec): (Insert hook, yo, draw lp through) in each of the sts indicated, yo, draw through all lps on hook.

Example of 2-sc dec

Half double crochet decrease (hdc dec): (Yo, insert hook, yo, draw lp through) in each of the sts indicated, yo, draw through all lps on hook.

Example of 2-hdc dec

Double crochet decrease (dc dec): (Yo, insert hook, yo, draw loop through, draw through 2 lps on hook) in each of the sts indicated, yo, draw through all lps on hook.

Example of 2-dc dec

Treble crochet decrease (tr dec): Holding back last lp of each st, tr in each of the sts indicated, yo, pull through all lps on hook.

Example of 2-tr dec

US		UK
sl st (slip stitch)	=	sc (single crochet)
sc (single crochet)	=	dc (double crochet)
hdc (half double crochet)	=	htr (half treble crochet)
dc (double crochet)	=	tr (treble crochet)
tr (treble crochet)	=	dtr (double treble crochet)
dtr (double treble crochet)	=	ttr (triple treble crochet)
skip	=	miss